River of Being

River of Being

A Parable for the Spiritual Journey

by Nathaniel Newby
with Shirley E. Knight

Illustrated by Ekaterina Ilina

RESOURCE *Publications* · Eugene, Oregon

RIVER OF BEING
A Parable for the Spiritual Journey

Copyright © 2022 Awake Now. All rights reserved. Except for brief quotations in critical publications or reviews, no part of this book may be reproduced in any manner without prior written permission from the publisher. Write: Permissions, Wipf and Stock Publishers, 199 W. 8th Ave., Suite 3, Eugene, OR 97401.

Resource Publications
An Imprint of Wipf and Stock Publishers
199 W. 8th Ave., Suite 3
Eugene, OR 97401

www.wipfandstock.com

PAPERBACK ISBN: 978-1-6667-3872-8
HARDCOVER ISBN: 978-1-6667-9978-1
EBOOK ISBN: 978-1-6667-9979-8

MARCH 14, 2022 8:14 AM

Contents

Acknowledgement | vii
Introduction | ix

A Parable for the Spiritual Journey | 1

The Human Experience | 4

Life in the Ocean | 4

Progressing up the River | 6
The Mouth of the River | 6
The Rapids | 9
The Pool | 11
Potential Traps | 11

The Base of the Falls | 12

Stuck in the Pool | 13

The Journey up the Waterfall of Being | 16

Phase 1 – Losing External Trappings | 16

Phase 2 – Emotional Turmoil | 18

Phase 3 – Dark Night of the Soul | 18

The Key Realization in the Waterfall of Being | 20

Above the Waterfall | 23

Visiting the Space Above the Falls | 23
Living Above the Falls | 24
A Quiet Place | 24
New Ways of Being | 24
Oneness in Action | 26

Beyond the Falls | 28

Level 1: Orientation | 28
Challenges as You Progress | 30
Level 2: Residency | 32
Level 3: Becoming | 34
Level 4: Active Unfoldment | 36

Using the Map | 39

Acknowledgement

Linda Starr, editor

Introduction

Who am I, where am I, and why am I here?

This book offers a map for the spiritual journey, particularly the far reaches that are not widely known. Maps give us distinctions so we can talk about where we are. Maps also allow us to discuss the path ahead.

Wherever you are, you are not lost, and you are not alone.

A Parable for the Spiritual Journey

Imagine you are a salmon swimming in the ocean. You go wherever the currents and food sources take you. Your focus is on day-to-day survival.

One day you notice a change. You feel a new desire, and you start going in a definite direction. You swim towards the river where you were spawned, the river that brought you to the sea. As you swim up that river, you leave the saltwater behind and begin to adjust to the freshwater.

Soon you encounter rapids where the current is strong. You are compelled to continue and coasting is not an option. After a while, the ocean is a distant memory, and you have no desire to return there.

On your journey, as you navigate the intermittent rapids, you learn skills and techniques. You gain strength, resilience, and competence. In each section of the river, you discover the energy you need to meet the challenges you encounter.

Some of the fish around you do not make it. They get stuck, caught, or devoured. Some get exhausted and stop trying. Some seem content to stay where they are.

Sooner or later, if you persist on your journey, you come to a large pool where you can rest. After catching your breath, you are ready to move on, so you dive confidently into the whitewater ahead. This time, instead of progressing, you are thrown back into the pool. You dive in again, and again you are thrown back. Water crashes down on you, and you get tumbled in the churning force.

You are strong, fit, and knowledgeable about the river so far. You have acquired skills and understanding, and yet you continue to get knocked back into the pool.

Finally you realize you are not encountering another set of rapids. You are now at a waterfall, and the only way up is to learn how to fly. Yes fly. You must propel yourself airborne to continue your progress.

If you make your way to the top of the waterfall but are disoriented and unstable, you get swept back down into the pool below.

If you stay above the waterfall, you find a quiet place to rest where you regain your strength and adjust to the new environment.

If you do not make it up the waterfall, you begin to notice that the pool is stagnant. You see salmon that did not journey onward, and you notice that they are rotting around you. You can forge on, or you can swim in circles in the pool.

The Ocean

The Human Experience

Life in the Ocean

The ocean is common everyday life where you are compelled by your senses and little else. Your conversations are about you and are centered on your personal self. You react to your environment without awareness of a broader, deeper, or higher perspective. Like everyone else in the ocean, you focus on things in the physical world and are concerned with appearances.

You are conscious of your immediate life, but you are aware of little else. You think this physical existence is all there is. Life lacks purpose, meaning, or direction. You live according to the beliefs of your family, culture, and media. You follow those whose beliefs align with your own, you defend those beliefs, and you feel threatened when others do not share your views.

At some point you realize there must be more to life than satisfying your senses or meeting other people's expectations. You become restless with the absence of passion in your life. You begin asking — Why is this happening to me? When you stop feeling like a victim and start taking responsibility, this is the beginning of awakening. You are gaining awareness.

The River

Progressing up the River

The Mouth of the River

You leave the ocean when you experience an interruption in your life. This involves a noteworthy event or turning point such as registering for a workshop, visiting a spiritual community, or outgrowing your social circle. It might involve facing a new challenge or opportunity such as moving to a new location or experiencing an illness. Anything that jolts you out of your routine or compels you to seek meaning can help you progress on your spiritual journey.

The transition point is that moment when you become aware of observations and insights that you previously did not notice. You realize you are conscious of your activities including thinking, choosing, using language, and taking action. You question old beliefs, and you begin discarding those that no longer fit. You sense that purpose and meaning are emerging. You awaken to possibility.

Once the change has happened, you will never be the same. Like the salmon, you are adapted to the freshwater now. You have left the saltwater behind.

As you progress up the river and overcome challenges, you will need to take time to rest and refresh periodically. Learning takes energy, so give yourself the opportunity to pause, appreciate, reflect, and adapt to new ways of being.

When you get a sense that it is time to move on, it is best to continue. Avoiding the call by resisting or refusing to progress leads to more intense ways to get your attention. The gentle prod becomes a noticeable push and then an even more forceful shove.

We all experience pain in life. Instead of living in agony about your agony, or living in misery about your misery, grieve authentically, be comforted by wholesome practices, and know that freedom is ahead on your journey into deeper insights and higher revelations.

The Rapids

The Rapids

Encountering rapids corresponds to growth and learning opportunities. You face rapids when you experience an impactful event, learn from an effective source, engage in an expansive experience, or make a significant change in your life.

Some rapids are more challenging than others. They can be fun, or they can nearly kill you. They can be a one-time activity or an ongoing pursuit. Some you move through quickly while others seemingly never end.

Your journey on the spiritual river is traditionally a multi-year process of self-help and personal growth. An experienced guide can help you navigate. Options abound for learning various tools, techniques, methodologies, and practices, so select whichever ones align with your interests and ways of being. All pathways of progression lead to the same space.

Between the rapids are peaceful sections of the river where you rest until you are compelled to continue. Once you traverse all the rapids, congratulations! You have completed the first section of the river.

The Pool

The Pool

You come to a large pool, which offers a welcome place to rest. At this point you are confidant and courageous. You are experienced at navigating the river, and you have grown stronger. You have made tremendous progress; however, beware of ways of getting sidetracked or ensnared.

Potential Traps

- Overconfidence: Just because you have progressed that does not mean you have all the answers. Achieving enlightenment is a process, and there is always more to learn than we can imagine.

- Sharing your enthusiasm: It is normal to feel excited and alive with new energy when you realize that your old life was shallow and devoid of meaningful direction. You will want to share your insights and bring others along on your journey. If people refuse to listen, or if they refuse to be moved by your discoveries, let them be as they are. People are not problems to be fixed. Trying to drag them into bliss is an interference and a source of frustration.

- Judging other people's progress: There are some human beings who will not enter the river in this lifetime. They are content swimming in the ocean. It is ineffective to judge anyone else's journey. Respect others wherever they are and keep moving. All levels of learning are valuable and are appropriate for those who are there.

- Becoming narrow minded: Teachers who are only aware of the entry phases of the spiritual journey may be heavy handed, restrictive, and narrowly focused, which can make progress more difficult than it needs to be. Instead of constricting to fit their approach, seek an open environment where you are allowed to question, discuss, and experiment. Learn what works for your particular ways of being.

When you are rested and ready, you continue your journey. You dive into the whitewater and get repelled. You dive in again and again are pushed back. After several attempts, you realize you are facing a challenge unlike any you have faced before.

The Base of the Falls

There is one waterfall on the spiritual river – the Waterfall of Being. The route you take to get there is not important. Maybe you challenged yourself by studying martial arts, running a business, or working in sales. Maybe you studied with a guru, read books, or earned certifications. Maybe you had amazing mystical experiences, or perhaps you have no concept of God whatsoever.

Your experiences are interesting, and it is engaging to compare notes with others; however, the water crashes down on all alike, no matter how you got there.

All pathways that involve taking responsibility for the content of your life and producing results with integrity lead to the Waterfall of Being. It does not matter what you believe or what you do not believe. The only activity that is important is that you arrive. The journey is universal to the human experience and reflects principles that operate with neither preference nor prejudice.

How to tell if you are at the base of the Falls:

1. Have you hit a wall? Has it become more difficult or impossible for you to produce results using techniques that worked for you in the past?
2. Are you unsatisfied and lethargic? Are you losing interest in pursuits that used to bring you joy? Are you asking — Is this all there is?
3. Have you outgrown the teachings you have studied? Are you eager to move on but see no place to go? Are you ready for new adventures?
4. Can you distinguish the major lessons you have learned on your journey, and do you feel complete with those lessons?

At the base of the Falls, you have two options:

1. Make it up the Waterfall of Being.
2. Rot in the pool below.

Returning to the ocean is not an option. Getting to the Falls is a one-way trip.

Stuck in the Pool

Trying to traverse the Waterfall with the same resources that helped you through the rapids keeps you stuck in the pool below. People who live at the base of the Falls without progressing tend to be bitter, disillusioned, cynical, and unreceptive to further learning. They feel they have done it all and know it all. They feel justified in critiquing and criticizing others.

The cynics may be well-respected, or at least they used to be. They feel they have reached as far as they could go, and yet they feel unsatisfied. Often, they are too proud to ask for help or guidance or to admit that they do not know something. They do not want to be seen as vulnerable, weak, or needy, and they get annoyed when it is revealed that they lack answers.

Life is about progressing in consciousness, so being stuck is contrary to Being. Sometimes people attach themselves to teachers who do not have a map for the advanced spiritual journey. These teachers take students as far as they are able, then they leave the students swimming in circles at the base of the Falls.

The Waterfall

The Journey up the Waterfall of Being

Just as the salmon cannot make it up the waterfall by swimming, so you can no longer progress on the spiritual river through your usual means. Like the salmon, you must learn how to fly, at least for brief intervals.

You fly by releasing attachment to who you thought you were. This means saying goodbye to anything and everything that is inauthentic, which often includes people, possessions, beliefs, ideals, dreams, and things you didn't even realize you were grasping. You fly by letting go of human limitations and allowing Being to emerge through you. Being is the Eternal expressing as actions and relationships.

On your spiritual journey you face opportunities and convert experiences into learning. What you learn is that life works most effectively when your personal self is not in charge. This means connecting with your conscience, your higher self, the source of Being. When you embrace new possibilities, you find that your greatest challenges provide the greatest potential for progress. In this progression, you turn learning into knowing and knowing into wisdom.

Three phases are recognizable as you learn to fly beyond your identification as a personal self.

Phase 1 – Losing External Trappings

In the first phase of your journey up the Waterfall of Being, your life begins to come apart, and what used to work for you no longer works. Maybe you have an intense breakthrough during a retreat. Maybe you are faced with a life-changing experience. There are many ways of being called to progress.

In the process you lose whatever you feel you possess such as your job, your status, and your marriage. You lose the things that have provided you with your personal identity. You are getting tossed around, and your life feels chaotic. You no longer know which way is up and which way is down.

Your ties to teachers and teachings unravel or are cut. You feel frustrated and misunderstood. You feel alone and ungrounded. You experience depths of loneliness you have never felt before. At times you may feel exhilarated by newfound freedom, but mostly you live in despair over loss until you collapse in complete exhaustion.

Sometimes you feel nostalgic for the old ways, both those that were effective and those that were ineffective. You look for the familiar when all is unfamiliar. Your old identity whispers that returning to the status quo is the best course of action.

You may be tempted to quit the journey because of the discomfort. Complaining and feeling sorry for yourself halts progress. There are only two choices for continuing as the human being you are: survive the journey and create a new life or rot in the pool below. Despite all the challenges, deep down you know that you need to keep moving forward.

Phase 2 – Emotional Turmoil

In the middle phase of the journey up the Waterfall of Being, nothing makes sense in your life. You see the risk ahead, but you do not yet see the reward. All the feelings you have repressed emerge with depth and intensity. Internal and external voices of blame, shame, guilt, and victimhood drown out other messages.

Anything you built on a flimsy foundation comes crashing down. You feel the weight of loss upon you. It is clear that your old life is gone, and you cannot retrieve it. People who do not understand the spiritual journey judge you as a failure and abandon you. You experience confusion and lack of direction.

Maybe you thought the spiritual journey was all about gentle sweetness. It's not, and this is your wake-up call. You begin to question everything. You lash out at convenient targets. You consider opting out of everything.

You are losing your old life, and you are gaining a new one. You are transforming so you can experience rebirth. The only way through it is through it. Sugarcoating, minimizing, avoiding, and latching on to false hopes will only delay your progress. This is a time to release your fears including your fear of flying.

Phase 3 – Dark Night of the Soul

The dark night of the soul is also known as the abyss or the Void. You no longer care about anything anymore, and you do not care that you do not care. You have exhausted your resources. Basically you are broken. Congratulations. You are closer to revealing the light you are.

In this phase, you lose your beliefs. You stop believing in your beliefs. This means you are no longer standing on inherited concepts and interpretations passed down through culture and community. You are becoming an empty vessel.

In this process, the darkness you carry emerges so you can learn from it. The key understanding you gain is equanimity. You learn that the dark and the light are equal, that the dark is not something to be dismissed, discounted, or avoided, as if you could.

You learn to see in the dark because even in darkness there is light. The light comes from within your own being. You develop night vision and make peace with darkness. You begin to look beyond the veil of your human persona and personality.

When you feel you have completely let go of the old you, an underlying fundamental attachment presents itself. This the linchpin — the core attachment on which you have built your life and your identity. Liberating the linchpin is also known as surrender. At this point your authentic self or your eternal self has replaced your personal self as the majority influence over your life.

This momentous milestone, which many have sought throughout human history, is also known as enlightenment. You are now on the path to pure joy. On this path your beliefs are replaced with the knowledge and wisdom you have gained while traversing the spiritual river.

You learn to coexist with polarities such as good/bad, right/wrong, true/false. You learn to accept life as it is instead of resisting it. You learn to love yourself as you are.

The Key Realization in the Waterfall of Being

In the Waterfall of Being you lose everything and enter Nothing. When you face the Nothing, you experience Being, which is the Eternal expressing as actions and relationships. From Being worlds emerge, and there is the possibility of everything. You discover the action of Being that brings forth creations. That action is language, creation language, language that is generative, language that sparks and coordinates action, language that says, "Let there be light, and there is light" (Genesis 1:3).

In the Waterfall you lose the attachments that keep you from progressing. This includes attachment to the story of your life so far. Your human accomplishments and all the facts of your biography are irrelevant in the Falls, although they do make for an interesting tale of transformation.

In the Waterfall of Being you realize that you exist without things. You exist without houses and computers and shoes. You exist beyond your human structure. You realize you can drop your stories about having *things* and instead focus attention on actions and relationships.

You realize you are not limited by what you perceive with your human senses. You are not limited to reactions you cannot control. You stop blaming others for your life.

Learning to navigate the Falls takes as long as it takes. You may fall back down into the pool repeatedly. You may feel like you have hit a boulder or are hurtling toward the mouth of a bear. The more baggage you carry, the more difficult the journey. The journey is a process of releasing.

Above the Waterfall

Above the Waterfall

Visiting the Space Above the Falls

When you have had an immersive, blissful, magical experience, there is a good chance you were visiting the space above the Waterfall of Being. The experience is also known as being in the zone. In that space you have amazing clarity and expansive awareness. You are in the flow of life, and everything unfolds with ease. You realize you are performing beyond your normal human construct.

You experience the space above the Waterfall of Being in those moments when you expand into harmony with life, when you feel no need to change or control anything, when your mind is quiet and your heart is full, when you are joyful about letting the moment be as it is.

The moment may be a peak experience such as holding a newborn baby, enjoying the wonder of nature, facing death, being in love, or feeling transported by art. In that moment you feel uncontained in your body, and you lose track of time and place.

When you are a surprised visitor to the space of Being, you are not aware of how you got there, how to stay, or how to return at will. Because the feeling is so fulfilling, you want to recreate the experience. You listen to the same piece of music or attend the same workshop again. You hike the same trail or try to remember what it felt like to be in love.

The spiritual journey involves graduating from visitor status. It involves learning to stabilize above the Falls without being pulled up, entranced, or entrained by rituals, scenery, or someone else's energy. It involves consciously connecting with Being, regardless of external conditions so that you live permanently above the Waterfall of Being.

Living Above the Falls

A Quiet Place

When you consciously make it up the Waterfall of Being, you have overcome many challenges. You have put in the work so that you are no longer a visitor. Take time to refresh your energy so you can learn new ways of being. For example, you will learn how to avoid being hooked and ensnared by your old life. An experienced guide can help you reflect, adjust, and avoid the common pitfalls. Above the Falls, whole new vistas open up, and you feel a sense of joy and fulfillment.

New Ways of Being

In this parable, the further below the Falls you are, the more your personal self is in charge of your life. Your personal self is ruled by your human senses and is only aware of living in this world where things appear and disappear. The further you progress beyond the Falls, the more you allow Being to unfold and emerge through you. Being is the joy of existence and the awareness of Oneness.

Below the Falls you are motivated by your wants, needs, emotions, and moods. You are driven by your beliefs and your desire for others to believe as you do. You react to life to protect yourself and to avoid being further wounded.

Above the Falls you are not attached to stories about being a victim or being unworthy. The result is you allow life to unfold organically. You no longer struggle to hide from, defend, impose, or fight for human limitations. Instead your actions proceed from your awareness of health, wholeness, joy, clarity, grace, and the availability of resources, which results in harmony.

The key activity that allows you to live above the Waterfall of Being is honesty — being honest with yourself about who you are and your relationship with Being. Your attention is no longer on your individual self. Instead it is on the field of operation, which is the space where you exist in relationships and are open to possibilities.

Living above the Waterfall of Being is often referred to as enlightenment. You can use the term *enBeingment* to emphasize consciously allowing Being to operate through you. You stop focusing on your individual limitations and connect with Oneness. In your actions and relationships people see that you address concerns and produce results that are considered valuable.

After getting acclimated, you either stay near the Waterfall where you assist other travelers, or you continue the journey. When you continue, you discover that the current in this section of the river is not as difficult as it was below the Falls, although it does present its own challenges. Now, however, you have developed the strength and the understanding to navigate effectively. Even though you have progressed in consciousness, you must still learn and exercise discernment to avoid pride and other pitfalls.

Oneness in Action

When you discard ineffective patterns and habits, you enter your new life. Most importantly, to live above the Waterfall of Being, you transcend the duality that is a fundamental characteristic of this universe. You transcend the true/false, right/wrong, good/bad conversations that people have below the Falls. These conversations dissolve in Oneness as you progress.

In other words, personal stories about what is right and wrong and good and bad are irrelevant beyond our individual notions. You realize that everyone is experiencing their own relative reality and that this is not a problem to be solved. With your insightful perspective you perceive wholeness and include polarities as well as the space in between.

Above the Falls, instead of focusing on having truth, you focus on effective action. Everything is energy, and you direct energy to promote well-being. You direct energy towards being who you came to be, to supporting existence, and to progressing in consciousness. You focus on bringing light to darkness.

Instead of operating as a limited human being, you begin operating as a divine being experiencing this universe of appearances. As you become aware of the Infinite and Eternal, you release attachment to gods and religions that are projections of human personalities. This includes gods who have value judgments about who is worthy and who is unworthy.

You realize that Oneness diversifies into Being creating the myriad of expressions we see such as you, me, worlds, galaxies, plants, animals, and people all over the planet. You realize that Oneness, Source, Eternal Consciousness is unlimited and unbounded. It just is forever without boundaries.

You realize that you are responsible for your actions, which includes your thoughts and your conversations. You learn that language is generative, that we create with language, and you begin choosing conversations with care and consciousness. This includes conversations with yourself.

You learn to develop your conscience and live by spiritual laws or laws of Being. You learn to focus on universal principles instead of getting enthralled by the personalities of teachers and leaders. You begin operating as the Eternal expressing as actions and relationships.

The more you progress, the more responsible you become. You are responsible for living in integrity with laws of Being.

Beyond the Falls

Four distinct levels are discernable beyond the Waterfall of Being. Understanding progression is useful because what is effective in one space may be ineffective in another. When your life is in order, and then you experience disorder, you may have advanced to the next space without realizing it. You may be operating at a new level without being aware that you are.

Similarly a person can operate very effectively in one aspect of life and not very successfully in other areas. For example, someone who is considered a virtuoso or a most-valuable player may not make a great teacher or coach. Knowing where you are on the spiritual river is helpful for understanding yourself and your relationship to life.

Successfully navigating the space above the Falls requires focusing attention, listening to conscience, and learning how to operate with laws of Being. Laws of Being are the principles for how existence expresses and relates in this universe. These spiritual principles are found in wisdom that is common across time and traditions.

Level 1: Orientation

The first space above the Waterfall of Being is orientation. Arriving there is similar to moving to a new city and beginning to get your bearings. You generally understand how life works in this new environment, and you begin to act appropriately. Instead of being driven to protect your personal identity, you start to consciously align with Being. You redirect your focus so that Being is the organizing principle of your life. Being is the revelation of Conscious Light in this universe.

As you move into awareness, you observe activities, including conversations in your own mind, without attacking and defending. You identify your feelings, needs, and standards and recognize their origin. You take responsibility for your actions and reactions, and you set aside your personal pride and insecurities.

You become tuned to your conscience and develop awareness of the space, which is the field where activities occur and are possible. You delve deeper into honesty and integrity, which results in deeper and higher realizations. As you focus on aligning with the structures of Being, you assist in maintaining well-being by recognizing the flows of the space.

Basically you learn to read energy. Everything is energy, and the flow of energy produces results. Operating appropriately to the space means seeing how people's beliefs, moods, and other activities are working separately and more importantly together. You learn to recognize impediments that affect the flow of energy, such as lying to yourself and others. The overall result of your alignment with Being is harmony.

The ability to consciously connect with Being at will requires commitment and practice. In your practice you learn to locate and reside in the Stillness or the Silence. You learn to use language consciously, to accurately identify concerns and to replace dualistic criticism, such as good/bad and better than/less than, with conversations about effective action. Effective action addresses concerns and promotes well-being. As you hone your abilities, you spend less and less time in frustration, confusion, and blame.

If you are serious about learning, you generally spend one to three months in orientation. If you are inattentive, you languish. The universe does not force you to progress. It is up to you to decide when to listen to conscience and when to take action. While you do not have to continue, there are consequences for not going when called. Consequences include feeling limited instead of fulfilled.

Challenges as You Progress

- Staying grounded: Your view of yourself and your world is changing, and you may feel untethered as you look for new reference points. To stay grounded, know that this world is not an illusion. This is a world where things appear and disappear according to the law of thought. The point of this life is not to be somewhere else or to discount this experience as fake. The point is to learn through the opportunities at hand.

- Maintaining Stillness: Living in society with its attendant distractions is challenging. This is why some people retreat to solitude and spiritual communities. Give yourself time and space to integrate what you are learning. We all need time to rest and reflect.

- Stabilizing: While you are getting oriented to this new space, you may visit your old life on occasion. You are sometimes still swayed by your personal desires and fears and by collective beliefs and moods. With practice you can learn not to get ensnared by the drama. For example, you can witness chaos without becoming chaotic. You can observe disorder without becoming disorderly. The key is to practice compassion, which means being able to enter into conversations without needing to change or control what is not yours to change or control.

- Developing clarity: Compassion is not the same as passivity. Sometimes effective action is not sweet and gentle; sometimes it is swift and decisive. For example, effective action involves setting clear boundaries so you can continue your progress, which may mean releasing people who are stagnant or disruptive.

- Encountering visitors: You may meet people who are visitors above the Waterfall of Being. They may know they are operating differently from how they did before, but they do not know why. When they are content going at their own pace, they may not welcome your interference. If someone is harmoniously in the flow of life one moment and then clearly upset and disrupted the next, likely they are not stabilized above the Falls. If a teacher does not like to be questioned, that can be a sign that they are just visiting and cannot articulate the activities of Being. Knowing what is happening alleviates confusion and disappointment.

- Maintaining perspective: Experiencing Oneness and harmony does not make you or anyone else any more special than you already are. While awareness of Being can produce incredible highs, reaching such a state does not exempt you or anyone else from ethics and morals. You are not the chosen one just because you have experienced the power, wonder, and wisdom of Being. Everyone is called, and everyone is chosen. If some choose not to go, do not take that personally. Just keep minding your own internal light.

Moving into new spaces can be challenging. Just as in other aspects of life, an experienced guide can help you navigate to make your journey easier. As you progress, your work will be revealed to you, and all that you need to fulfill your duties and responsibilities will be made available to you.

Level 2: Residency

Progressing into the second space above the Waterfall of Being is like becoming a citizen of a country instead of just being a tourist. You understand the culture, and you know your way around to a sufficient degree. Results emerge through you more naturally, including results that seem highly synchronistic to others. You feel at home and comfortable above the Waterfall of Being, you operate with much less personal focus than before, and you often meet the moment with grace and ease. You are now operating properly with the space of Being. You are taking action that is *proper to the space.*

You are consciously aware of affecting the space of operation. You are aware that your conduct produces results. Frequently you act with congruency, consistency, and coherency within your sphere of operation, which means you live in the flow of life.

You understand the relationships of entities, and you are integral to the movement of energy within the space of those relationships. You progress energy patterns effectively, and the energy you move through the system becomes part of the sphere of operation. You know you are acting in cooperation with universal forces and not by your own personal means and methods.

When you live in residency above the Waterfall of Being, you are aware that Consciousness is expressing through you and as you. You become aware that you are listening to conscience and that your conscience is your divine connection between your human being and your spiritual being. Your personal foibles, pitfalls, and prejudices are minimized. Instead, you connect with Being, which is continually emerging from Source, Eternal Consciousness, the Unbounded Is.

This is the stage at which you are traditionally considered a guru or luminary. In business and the arts you are considered a master in your field. Designers whose creations feel natural, intuitive, wholesome, compelling, and revelatory are producing results from this level of Being. Their name or their brand becomes synonymous with a design, a fashion, a movement, an art area, or an innovation.

The further along you are on your journey, the more distant you become from your former life. People below the Falls may find you aloof, disinterested, or even condescending. You find that you enjoy your own company more than you enjoy interacting with tedious people. If you feel lonely at this point, know that the narrowing of the way is part of the process. As you continue to connect with Oneness, you enjoy the wholesomeness of life and realize that you are never alone.

No matter what you are experiencing, it is helpful to practice compassion, which is the ability to generate another person's conversation from their experience while still maintaining your own identity. It is effective to be able to converse with others without becoming entangled and without acting superior. Although you have achieved an advanced level in residency, it is important to be able to interact effectively with the everyday world as needed.

When you are proper to the space, you begin operating with wisdom more often than you did before. Wisdom helps you navigate new spaces and understand new possibilities. With wisdom you move in proper relationship with the universe. You are consciously an Awakened Being. You may feel content with the magic you are creating. You may even feel complacent, and yet there is more ahead.

Level 3: Becoming

In the third space above the Waterfall of Being you feel like you have become one with the universe. You realize that your human self is a structure that allows you to exist in this physical experience, and that your senses, your personality, your feelings, and all other human constructs are in service to Being. Your human structures allow you to navigate the space of this universe, and your focus is on Oneness expressing as actions and relationships. When you live this way, you are operating *as the space*.

Before this can happen, you must traverse the barrier between level 2 and level 3. Hitting the barrier can feel confusing and disorienting similar to experiencing a small waterfall. You may feel like you have graduated to a peaceful existence, and then without warning you encounter a challenge that is unique to the barrier. The challenge involves operating consistently with your human self in service to your divine self. Use your spiritual practices to filter through the barrier. Use the wisdom you have gained to navigate and operate effectively so you can continue your progress.

When you progress, you find that level 3 is a pivot point. It is an adjustment period where you transition to consciously embodying your spirit-being in your human form. You focus on clearing out the residue of your old beliefs and patterns. You hone your internal awareness, and you practice non-interference both with yourself and others. This means you allow what is to be as is without resorting to conflict, friction, and resistance.

You cultivate understanding for how this universe works, and you are aware of laws of Being. You realize that you are spiritual law in action, and harmony results from this understanding.

Choices fade, and you meet the moment with grace and ease. You effectively use your internal compass to feel into how to be effective in the moment and in the situation. Because your internal operations are directed by Being, you produce inspired results.

You nurture space by operating honestly and with integrity. You extend the space of operation by consciously operating from the harmony of Being. You create space where others can enjoy the emergence and revelation of Being if they so choose, space where people feel connected and transformed.

Often you become quiet. You generally exist in Stillness, and you may seem to fade into the background because of the calm you embody. You no longer require attention and validation from other people, and you are loud only when the situation calls for volume. Although you can access great power, you generally choose not to make a display of it. When and if you are recognized, you are recognized for wisdom.

Level 4: Active Unfoldment

Unfoldment is allowing Being to express through you. It involves using the operations of Being to upgrade and enhance structures in the world, which leads to the results we experience.

Unfoldment can also be thought of as *being the space* or as being the field. This is what Buddhists call becoming an empty vessel. You start to authentically experience yourself as Consciousness. You operate as the space and are for the most part, indistinguishable from the space. This happens when you are in the flow of life, and time and awareness of your human self disappears.

At times throughout your spiritual journey, you have likely allowed unfoldment to happen. At level 4 your approach to it changes. Prior to this space you produced results through passive unfoldment, which means you were waking up to realizations, and you spoke in terms of what you did.

In space 4 you are active, which means you are consciously unfolding. You generate results, not from the personal approach, but through awareness of universal processes. In this aspect, you actively allow space to be generated through you.

You work with proper distinctions about the operations of the universe, distinctions about the effects and the results of actions and relationships. In other words you understand the laws of Being that govern this existence, and you consciously embody these principles as your life. You are often recognized as a healer, a teacher, or both.

The River of Being

Using the Map

The parable of the salmon navigating the river on the journey home gives us language and distinctions for discussing experiences at the different stages of progression. Being able to pinpoint yourself on a map usually leads to clarity. You see how far you have come, and you see that the challenges you are facing are appropriate for where you are. You see the underlying beauty and integrity of the process even when the terrain is difficult to traverse. As you learn to appreciate the challenges, you gain wisdom.

While your individual journey is unique, it is also universal. Any route you take, any teacher you follow, any practice you adopt will lead you to the Waterfall of Being provided that route is grounded in honesty and integrity. You are not alone on this journey even though sometimes it feels like you are.

Experienced guides are available to assist you along the way. Assisting does not mean pushing you, pulling you, usurping your power, or keeping you stuck. On the journey you must learn to follow your conscience and take full responsibility for your life and all the results you experience.

There will be times when you are resting and times when you are progressing rapidly. Pace yourself by taking time to recuperate between the intervals of high activity.

No matter where you are, your journey of awakening will ultimately lead to balance, harmony and the joy of Being. On this journey you will overcome many challenges. May this map give you confidence as you progress.

∞